Approaches
to Politics

Approaches to Politics

Pierre Elliott Trudeau

Introduction by Ramsay Cook
Prefatory Note by Jacques Hébert

Translated by I. M. Owen

Toronto Oxford University Press *1970*

Contents

3/29/71 - pub - $1.84

Introduction

By RAMSAY COOK

The coming of the Quiet Revolution

On 20 June 1956 Maurice Duplessis's Union Nationale party was returned to power for the third consecutive time since 1944. The victory was a bitter blow for the growing forces of emancipation in Quebec, and especially for the provincial Liberal party. Georges-Émile Lapalme, who had stepped out of federal politics to assume the provincial leadership in 1950, had worked vigorously to rebuild his party after the defeat of 1952.[1] He had established an independent provincial organization, the Quebec Liberal Federation, and attempted to introduce democratic practices within the party. A newspaper, *La Réforme*, edited by Jean-Louis Gagnon, carried the party's message to a growing list of party faithful and provided a forum for the discussion of a variety of proposals for reform in the political, educational, social, and economic structure of Quebec society. The party's program in 1956 reflected this new philosophy. It proposed increased agricultural subsidies, extensive educational reform, liberalized labour legislation, and more stringent controls over foreign capital in the development of

---

[1] Georges-Émile Lapalme, *Le Bruit des choses réveillées: mémoires* (Montréal, 1969).

natural resources. Yet, when the votes were counted on
the night of June the 20th, the Union Nationale had
actually increased its standing in the Legislature, while
the Liberals' total dropped from twenty-three at dissolu-
tion to twenty in the new house.[2] It looked as though the
age of Duplessis would never end.

The 1956 election suggested two general conclusions
to Quebeckers who opposed the Duplessis régime. The
first was that the Union Nationale machine was more
powerful even than anyone had suspected. The second
conclusion drawn by an increasingly large group of
people was that as long as the opposition remained frag-
mented—there had been candidates from the provincial
CCF or PSD, from the Labour Progressive party, two independent nationalists and a host of other independents in
the 1956 election—there could be no certainty of defeat-
ing the Duplessis party. These conclusions were obvious.
But what was more difficult was to devise ways both of
cracking the power of the Union Nationale machine and
of formulating a basis for coalition among disparate
opposition groups.

The power of the Duplessis machine lay, at least super-
ficially, in its unlimited use of patronage and its willing-
ness to practise corruption and intimidation during
elections. Shortly after the 1956 election two priests,
Abbé Gérard Dion and Abbé Louis O'Neill, both of Laval
University, published a stinging condemnation of what
they called 'Political Immorality in the Province of Quebec' in a little-known clerical publication, *Ad Usum
Sacerdotum*. The article, soon picked up by *Le Devoir*
and broadcast across the province and the country, zeroed
in on two kinds of political tactic: intellectual blackmail
and plain vote buying. The first took the form of building

---

[2] Vincent Lemieux, *Quatre Élections provinciales au Québec*
(Québec, 1970), 6-10.

the myth of the communist menace and the Ottawa menace, sometimes linked together. The second included
patronage, violence on election day, telegraphing votes,
and numerous other carefully devised methods of ensur-
ing the desired outcome at the ballot box. But what was
worse than the practices themselves, Dion and O'Neill
insisted, was that they were accepted, almost without a
whisper of criticism, by a large number of Quebeckers.
'The danger is all the greater,' they wrote, 'because a
great deal of evidence shows that the consciences of the
faithful and even those of members of religious orders
no longer experience any feeling of scandal when con-
fronted with such corruption.'[3]

But why was a people so easily corruptible and so
readily intimidated? Four years later, early in 1960, a
teaching brother, soon to be famous as Frère Untel,
attempted an answer to the question: 'We are afraid of
authority; we live in a climate of magic, where under
penalty of death we must infringe no taboo, where we
must respect all of the formulae, all of the conformities.'[4]
The faithful French-Canadian Catholic, obedient to his
Church, had transferred his unquestioning loyalty to
matters of politics. And politicians, traditionally, had
found this a useful condition to encourage. It made their
main objective—holding office—so much simpler. Since
Quebec was the only province in which the French Canadians were a majority, skilful politicians could play upon
Quebeckers' fears that their culture and language would
be threatened by the majority unless unquestioning support was given a party which represented the national
needs. Maurice Duplessis was a master of appealing to
his people's insecurities, and of intertwining religious and

[3] Gérard Dion and Louis O'Neill, *Two Priests Censure Political
Immorality in Quebec* (Montreal, 1956), 16.
[4] *Les Insolences du Frère Untel* (Montréal, 1960), 16.

cultural concerns. In 1948 he had asserted a theme which
he repeated consistently as the justification for his poli-
cies. 'The legislature of Quebec is a fortress,' he insisted,
'that we must defend without failing. It is that which
permits us to construct the schools which suit us, to speak
our language, to practise our religion and to make laws
applicable to our population.'[5] Here was an appeal to a
state-of-siege mentality.

But there was more than this insecurity at the root of
the French Canadian's apparent acceptance of immorality
in politics. Historically, many French Canadians had developed an attitude toward government which combined
the conception of the paternalistic provider with an opposition to state intervention in society's affairs. Thus the
government, or rather the party in power, was expected
to provide jobs at least for its supporters and dole out
contracts and local improvements to loyal constituencies.
But that same state was warned constantly to keep its
nose out of matters like education and social security,
which were, after all, religious not political duties.

Each of these apparently contradictory attitudes
stemmed from a view of government and the state as
something external to, even foreign to, French-Canadian
society. The French Canadian's traditional conception of
authority was hierarchical, from the top down, not egali-
tarian or democratic. Mgr L.-A. Pâquet, a distinguished
French-Canadian theologian, summed up this view very
well when he wrote that 'all authority other than God's
own comes from divine authority. . . . The idea of authority born of the free will of man, and constituted according to human calculations alone, has thrown into the
world a social conception which is only a cause of trouble
and a source of instability. . . . What must not be ad-

---

[5] Cited in H. F. Quinn, *The Union Nationale* (Toronto, 1963),
117-18.

mitted, is that the people itself is sovereign, and that, in choosing the members of a legislative assembly, it delegates to them the power to govern.'[6]

It was this conception of authority, more than anything else, which allowed corrupt electoral habits to develop in Quebec. Since authority came from on high rather than from the people themselves, its actions were hardly matters of individual responsibility. And so, as Gérard Filion wrote after the 1956 election, 'Most of the people in Quebec seem to have two consciences, one for their private lives, the other for their public life. . . . Lying, cheating, stealing is hateful when one is engaged personally but when done in the name of a Party, a Deputy, or one's Government, it is innocent, in fact almost considered as an act of virtue.'[7]

If this attitude toward authority explained, on the philosophical level, Duplessis's apparently unbreakable hold on power, the divisions within the opposition were nearly as important on the strategic level. Quebec was certainly not monolithic in its support of the Union Nationale; even in 1956 that party had obtained only fifty-one per cent of the popular vote, which was more than it had received in any post-war election. The Liberals were the largest opposition group, assured of at least forty per cent of the voters' support. The PSD, the Quebec wing of the CCF, had made a significant impact upon a small circle of intellectuals but had failed to penetrate the masses. This did not mean that the labour unions were happy with the existing political situation. Duplessis's restrictive labour laws and obvious favouritism toward big business made the unions, especially the Catholic Unions, potential supporters of political change. There was also

---

[6] Cited in Camille Laurin, 'Autorité et personalité au Canada français', in *Ma Traversée du Québec* (Montréal, 1970), 21.
[7] *Le Devoir*, 8 août 1956.

an important wing of the Roman Catholic Church, epitomized by Father Georges-Henri Lévesque and the School of Social Sciences at Laval, which was more than ready to reject the religious conservatism that lay at the basis of the traditional French-Canadian nationalism. Then there was that group loosely termed 'intellectuals'. Some were nationalists, but of a new school. At *Le Devoir* the leadership of André Laurendeau and Gérard Filion was designed to turn that paper's nationalism in a left-ward direction: to take up the cause of the labour unions, to demand educational reform, to support plans for better social welfare programs, and, above all, to denounce the corruption of the Duplessis administration. ('*Le Devoir* is a bolshevik newspaper,' Duplessis remarked in 1954.[8]) Less nationalist, even anti-nationalist, but more liberal, even socialist, was the group of intellectuals that expressed themselves through the little magazine, *Cité libre*.

The central figure in the *Cité libre* group was Pierre Elliott Trudeau. Since the beginning of the 1950s he and his friends had been propounding one basic idea about the fundamental weakness of Quebec society. That idea was the lack of democracy in Quebec. By the mid-fifties, and especially after Duplessis's victory in 1956, the *cité-libristes*, and especially Trudeau, began seriously to develop a strategy to unite the opposition forces in order to defeat the Union Nationale and launch Quebec on a course of democratic reform.

Perhaps the *citélibristes* could be called the 'philoso-phes' of the 'quiet revolution'. Their function was to de-mystify traditional beliefs and instructions, to unmask the authoritarianism, clericalism, and corruption of the *ancien régime* and to prepare the way, intellectually, for its overthrow. Pierre Juneau, Gérard Pelletier, Charles Lussier, and the others who helped start *Cité libre* would

---

[8] Ibid., 14 janvier 1954.

all have agreed with Pierre Trudeau's exhortation in the first issue of the magazine. 'We wish to testify to the Christian and French fact in North America,' Trudeau wrote. 'So be it: but let us make a *tabula rasa* of all the rest. It is necessary to submit to methodical doubt all of the political categories that the previous generation bequeathed to us: the strategy of resistance is no longer useful for the full flowering of the city. The time has come to borrow from the architect that discipline called "functional", to cast into the nettles the thousand prejudices with which the past encumbers the present, and build for the new man. Let us overthrow the totems, break the taboos. Or better, let us consider them cancelled. Coldly, let us be intelligent.'[9]

Through the pages of *Cité libre*, at the sessions of the newly founded *Institut Canadien des Affaires publiques* —Quebec's Couchiching, founded in the fifties—over Radio-Canada, and wherever else the opportunity offered, Trudeau and his friends preached a consistent message: the great need of Quebec was a large infusion of democratic thinking. The old concept of authority, from on high, had to be replaced with a new philosophy: the doctrine of popular sovereignty. If democracy could be achieved, all else would follow: educational reforms enacted, social and economic planning begun, and corruption ended. The spirit of Duplessis and the spirit of democracy were sworn enemies. 'Democracy first' became Trudeau's rallying cry and one behind which he hoped he could help to unite all of the forces opposed to the Union Nationale in Quebec.

The obvious step for Trudeau and his friends would have been to unite with the Liberal party. But that was not possible. For all that they admired Lapalme's efforts

---

[9] Pierre Elliott Trudeau, 'Politique fonctionnelle', *Cité libre*, juin 1950, 21.

to democratize the party and give it a modern program, Trudeau and his friends suspected that a large segment of the party was as traditionalist as the Union Nationale and, if in power, far from immune to anti-democratic and corrupt proceedings. 'I cannot help admiring the tenacity of the small group of men who set out to infuse some democratic blood into the veins of a party which has never been anything more than a syndicate of the private interests,' was the way that Trudeau expressed his somewhat skeptical attitude to the Liberals in 1956.[10]

Instead the effort was made, in September 1956, to launch the Rassemblement, an organization whose somewhat vague objective was to build 'a movement of education and democratic action'. Pierre Dansereau, of the University of Montreal, was its first president, Trudeau vice-president. Its constitution and declaration of purpose was lengthy and detailed. But its first principle was an explicit statement of the doctrine of popular sovereignty and its clear implication: 'Men live in society in order that each individual can realize himself to the maximum. The only justification for political authority is to permit the establishment and development of an order which will favour this realization.' And the last of its general principles underlined the point again. 'A true political conscience will be born only at the instigation of a vast political education movement which will make the people conscious of their powers and put them in a well-established position to exercise them.'[11]

There was something rather too academic about the Rassemblement. It held its meetings, argued over ideology and strategy, but it lacked a power base. Gérard Bergeron, who sympathized with the aims of the group, described a typical member this way: 'Politically, he is a

---

[10] *Vrai*, 3 novembre 1956.
[11] *Le Devoir*, 14 septembre 1956.

worried, bitter, aimless man. The social force which he represents has no political expression. It operates in a vacuum.'[12] Trudeau was not prepared to accept this assessment. In October of 1958 he prepared a long manifesto—'A Democratic Manifesto'—which was a call for all the divided opposition forces to come together to fight for democracy. 'Democracy first,' he declared. 'After that it will be up to the sovereign people to opt freely for the choices they prefer.'[13]

Nothing better expresses the philosophy of the Rassemblement than the series of articles Trudeau wrote for Jacques Hébert's journal *Vrai* during 1958 under the title 'Les Cheminements de la Politique'. *Vrai* was the organ of the Civic Action League, which had been organized to cleanse the notably corrupt politics of the City of Montreal. The movement was closely allied with the social nationalists of *Le Devoir* and its first leader, like the editor of *Le Devoir*, was a one-time member of the Bloc Populaire. This was Jean Drapeau, who was elected mayor of Montreal in 1954. Three years later, Drapeau was defeated when the Union Nationale openly supported his opponent. *Vrai*, founded in 1956, was a sparkling and pugnacious newspaper. It could not have been otherwise under the editorship of Jacques Hébert. The journal's style was polemical, its cause the underdog. Though occasionally spiced with polemic, Trudeau's almost professorial articles on the true source of political authority and the virtues of democracy struck a somewhat calmer note than was usual for the paper. But what is most impressive about these journalistic pieces is the ease with which obvious erudition is transformed into

[12] Gérard Bergeron, 'Political Parties in Quebec', *University of Toronto Quarterly*, April 1958, 366.

[13] Pierre Elliott Trudeau, 'Un Manifest démocratique', *Cité libre*, octobre 1958, 21.

clear, simple statements of fundamental political philosophy. He stated the essence of his argument early in the
series in a paragraph that illustrates the style and logic
of his mind. 'Human societies, then, differ from beehives
in that men are always free to decide what form of
authority they will adopt, and who will exercise it. And
it really is men who have the responsibility of taking
these decisions—not God, Providence, or Nature. In the
last analysis, any given political authority exists only
because men consent to obey it. In this sense, what exists
is not so much the authority as the obedience.'

This series, like 'The Democratic Manifesto', was the
platform upon which Trudeau hoped to launch a political
coalition strong enough to defeat the Union Nationale. At
the end of 1958 the Rassemblement, with Trudeau as
president, resolved to open discussions with other political and educational groups that shared the goal of 'democracy first'. The time seemed ripe, for the two labour
organizations, the Canadian Congress of Labour and the
Quebec Federation of Labour, had indicated their intention to join in the establishment of a 'new party', while
the Quebec Liberals had recently passed a resolution
calling for the union of all democratic organizations.
Thus, the Rassemblement was prepared to join these
forces and to enter directly into political action.[14]. Three
months later a group of twenty-one well-known Quebec
intellectuals representing the Liberals, the PSD, the Civic
Action League, the unions, and the universities launched
an appeal for unity among the opposition parties.[15]
Trudeau was among them.

This Union des forces démocratiques, despite its prom-
ising beginning, ultimately came to nothing. Within the
group ideological quarrelling and the unwillingness of

---

[14] *Le Devoir*, 1er décembre 1958.
[15] Ibid., 11 avril 1959.

some of the constituent parts to sink their identity in the common cause proved enfeebling. Outside political events were moving too quickly. The ice jam created by sixteen years of Union Nationale rule was breaking up. In 1957 the federal Liberal party had suffered defeat at the hands of John Diefenbaker. Maurice Duplessis could no longer tar the provincial Liberals with the federal centralist brush. More particularly Jean Lesage was freed from his Ottawa duties to assume the leadership of the Quebec Liberals. Then in September 1959 Maurice Duplessis died while touring Northern Quebec. At once the régime began to crumble, though at first it was held together, and even showed signs of renewal, under Paul Sauvé. But within three months Sauvé suffered a fatal heart attack. When the party faced the electorate, divided and tired, under the leadership of Antonio Barrette in June 1960, its great days were over. 'The Union Nationale is a man without a party,' Gérard Bergeron had written in 1958. 'That is its strength and its weakness. The provincial Liberals constitute a party without a man. That is their weakness without being a strength.'[16] In two short years, two elections and two deaths had changed all that.

In 1960 the Liberals had united all the opposition forces. The PSD ran no one. Pierre Laporte, once an independent nationalist of the *Le Devoir* variety, had joined the Liberal camp, as had René Lévesque, who was both more left and more nationalist than traditional Liberals. Yet one group was notably absent, though no one commented on it at the time. These were the men of *Cité libre*. Their political force had never been great. Their writings remained as proof of a major contribution to the coming of the 'quiet revolution'. But after 1960 Trudeau and his friends seemed fated for the calm life of the

---

[16] Gérard Bergeron, op. cit., 356.

university, the editorial chair, the trade union central, the law firm, or the civil service. Or so it appeared.

For Trudeau, at least, the years of the fifties were of fundamental importance. They were the years when he thought through and elaborated his political philosophy: the nature of authority, the strength of democracy, the value of federalism, the role of the state in economic life, the function of trade unions, the place of the Church, the dangers of nationalism, and the fundamental importance of individual liberty. But he learned also about the mechanics of politics. The Rassemblement and the Union des forces démocratiques failed in the short run. But the experience probably taught Trudeau that founding a new party was far more difficult than assuming control of an old one. It was a lesson he remembered when he once again set out on *Les Cheminements de la Politique.*

Prefatory note

By JACQUES HÉBERT

In 1958 I was editing a small weekly called *Vrai*—we had no doubts of the aptness of the title!—whose contributors included men as unlike each other as Gérard Pelletier and Victor Barbeau, Roland Parenteau and Abbé Pierre, René Lévesque and Pierre Trudeau, not to mention many young journalists who have since distinguished themselves in the press and in broadcasting.

When I have occasion to look up a date or check a recollection in the two thousand or so yellowing pages, I feel some slight embarrassment. Without repudiating the ideal that inspired us during the dark years of Duplessism, I feel a lively regret for botched texts, ill-judged tactics, furious attacks on people who were chiefly guilty of belonging to a generation that we were bound to oppose as a matter of course. In contrast, some articles are still shockingly relevant, as if nothing had happened in Quebec for twelve years, as if our people—distrustful as they are of ideas, first and last—must be incessantly reminded of certain truths that are never really listened to, and certainly never understood.

Unquestionably pre-eminent among these articles are those of a former *Vrai* contributor who has since become prime minister of Canada. A dozen years ago, Pierre Trudeau was not—it must be repeated yet again!—the young idler described to us by ignorant or disingenuous

scribblers. Even though his family circumstances would
have allowed him to succeed in life with less effort than
others, he had chosen the hard way—a long university
preparation that took him from Harvard to the London
School of Economics, by way of the Paris School of Political Science. Barrister and economist, in his full panoply of
diplomas, he had his choice of fields in which to make his
mark. But Pierre Trudeau had not finished his studies. It
was necessary for him to verify in the field the ideas he
had acquired, to compare actual life with his teachers'
theories about man and society. In other words, he had to
go around the world. He could have travelled as a tourist,
he could have afforded luxurious hotels. But he preferred
to go through Europe on a motorcycle, to walk along the
dusty roads of Africa with his pack on his back, to cross
India in a third-class carriage—an inquisitive and frater-
nal traveller discovering the world of human beings by
walking with the humble. (There is, in fact, no other
way.)

After he came back to this country, Pierre Trudeau
assigned himself a two-year stint in Ottawa (1949-51) as
economic adviser to the Privy Council. Without realizing
it, he was setting the stage intelligently for his dazzling
return to the federal capital; but it was Quebec that he
wanted to serve more directly, first because he was a
Quebecker and a French Canadian to the core, and secondly because it was obvious at that time that nowhere
else in the country were the rights of man so trodden on,
nowhere else was democracy so openly flouted. At home
in Montreal, Pierre Trudeau wanted to teach in the
Faculty of Law or the Faculty of Social, Economic, and
Political Science; but the doors of the University of Montreal were closed to him, for fear of incurring the wrath
of Duplessis. How fortunate we were, that we could
afford to dispense with his abilities!

This impatient man would have had every right to lose patience and choose another university, another city, another province. In fact, throughout the exasperating fifties this impatient man was to display the most exemplary patience, working in the shadows, immersing himself in labour law because Quebec lacked experts in this field and the workers were in dire need of defence against a reactionary, anti-union régime. Free, rich, athletic, a lover of life—as is so often underlined!—Pierre Trudeau worked with the dedication of a Benedictine, never succumbing to the lure of the ski-slopes until he had given his best to the preparation of remarkable memoranda on behalf of a union headquarters or a commission of inquiry.

Research, study, and reading never made Pierre Trudeau remote from the world of action. This intellectual played an active part in all the movements that then constituted the sole effective opposition to the régime. In 1950, with Gérard Pelletier and a few friends, he founded *Cité libre*; in 1956, he launched the Rassemblement; in 1958, he brought about the Union des forces démocratiques. Whenever a committee was formed for the defence of an imperilled civil liberty, for the release of an obscure citizen who had been illegally imprisoned, or against the proliferation of nuclear weapons, every time Pierre Trudeau was there; always he was the most effective member of the committee. In his leisure time—and I know no man of his generation who allowed himself so little—he contributed to learned journals. And once, for a popular journal, he wrote these *Approaches to Politics*.

At this time, when the younger generation believes that it has invented confrontation; when some set themselves up as defenders of the rights of man, often rightly but sometimes with the air of being the discoverers of the New World; when others call our political structures in question with loud shouts, as if it were not the simple duty of the democratic citizen to do just that; in this dynamic but dangerous climate, I thought it might be useful to draw to the attention of those who, in their agitation, have not yet altogether rejected reflection, these reflections on liberty, the dignity of man, and the art of confrontation.

Those who are unacquainted with Pierre Trudeau will perhaps insinuate that he would like to repudiate his writings of yesterday. Without seeking to convince extreme partisans, let me say to others that if that were so Pierre Trudeau would simply have refused me his permission to collect them in this little book.

Furthermore, he left me complete freedom to cut out any paragraphs that for one reason or another might have less interest than when they first appeared. In 1958 Pierre Trudeau was writing newspaper articles; he took account of topical matters, even sometimes interrupting the thread of his thought to reply to a detractor in the pamphleteering style that was his trademark. Would a more particular publisher have suppressed these allusions to people who have lost all influence in Quebec, or events that are no longer significant to the young reader of today? For my part, I was determined to publish the complete text of this series of articles, which appeared in *Vrai* from 15 February to 5 July 1958. My reason was precisely that I enjoy these references to the events of a still recent epoch—and find it significant that these scourges of Pierre Trudeau's ideas, clergy or laity, hurling their anathemas from the height of prestigious tribunes, should a dozen years later be great unknowns. It is also a convenient way of preventing the critics from saying that the publisher has expurgated from the work everything that might have embarrassed the author in 1970!

1 Government by mediocrities

The heaviest penalty for declining to engage in politics is to be ruled by someone inferior to yourself. PLATO

Tomorrow morning, preferably in the small hours, any one of you may be arrested and indicted in the courts on a charge of having assassinated the Grand Sultan. Your hearing will begin; a single witness will testify, in three short sentences, that you are mentally ill. Nobody will ask your opinion—after all, you are insane—and at the request of the Crown the judge will send you to rot in jail.

You find that bizarre? You think I am exaggerating? Far from it. With only minor variations, the thing happened before my eyes a few weeks ago.

I was in court that morning when a man appeared for trial on a charge of perjury. The Crown made no attempt to prove the accusation. One witness testified that he had seen the accused one day, at a distance, and that in his opinion the man had schizophrenia. This witness had not been properly sworn; nor had he established that he was a member of the college of physicians. The accused had no opportunity to defend himself or to cross-examine the witness. The whole thing happened very quickly, amidst considerable hubbub, and at some distance from the accused—who suddenly found himself being led to the cells.

This man, who had slept in his own bed the night before, who had come to court a free man and was expecting to go peacefully home, had to spend the ensuing weeks in the wing of Bordeaux Prison reserved for suspected dangerous criminals. And goodness knows how long he would have vegetated there if a lawyer named Benno Cohen had not worked for a writ of *habeas corpus*, and if a judge like the Hon. Roger Ouimet had not had enough regard for civil liberties to order his release.

Just have powerful enough enemies, or be obscure enough yourself, and you too can have this experience some day. We are appalled to think that in the days of absolute monarchy a *lettre de cachet* could send free men to penal servitude with no other form of trial. But does it appal us enough that similar things continue to happen in the democratic society we live in?

We give politicians the power of life and death over us; we authorize them to send us to war, imprison us, tax us, regulate our activity, expropriate our houses, discipline our children, supervise our conduct, our reading, and our speech. We let these men make the laws that restrict us, direct the policemen who arrest us, choose the lawyers who prosecute us, appoint the judges who sentence us. They can amend the constitution so as to postpone elections indefinitely and declare their government eternal; they can abolish the legal safeguards (injunction, prohibition, *mandamus*, *certiorari*, *quo warranto*) that protect our liberties; they can even abolish *habeas corpus*, or make it ineffective—as was actually done some fifteen years ago.

And we absent-mindedly bestow these absolute powers over our lives and welfare on a handful of men, in elections dominated by fanaticism and gangsterism, generally without asking of them the smallest guarantee of intelligence or of elementary honesty. Should one of them happen to overstep the bounds, we allow him to be made a judge, or a legislator for life in one of our upper houses.

The price of liberty, say the English, is eternal vigilance. But to be vigilant one must be aware of one's rights. It is important, then, to know what our freedom is founded on, and how far the state has authority to restrict it. In other words, strict limits must be placed on the right of one man to rule another. This indeed is the domain of politics. It is not, perhaps, excessive to devote a few articles in a weekly to the subject.

2 When madmen think they are ministers and MPs

We can only think of Plato and Aristotle in grand academic robes. They were decent fellows, like others, laughing with their friends; and when they diverted themselves with writing their Laws and their Politics they did it for their own amusement. This was the least philosophical, the least serious, part of their lives; the most philosophical part was to live simply and quietly. If they wrote of politics, it was as if to make rules for a lunatic asylum. And if they made a show of speaking of great affairs it was because they knew that the madmen they were talking to thought they were kings and emperors. They entered into their principles in order to mitigate as far as possible the damage done by their madness. PASCAL

We are going to be governed whether we like it or not; it is up to us to see to it that we are governed no worse than is absolutely necessary. We must therefore concern ourselves with politics, as Pascal said, to mitigate as far as possible the damage done by the madness of our rulers.

The first—almost the only—question to ask is: how does it happen that one man has authority over his fellows?

Sermons and worthy books are always talking of respect for the human personality and of the inviolability of conscience. In the context of our Christian civilization, those phrases have no meaning unless all men are regarded as fundamentally free and equal, each man being of infinite value in himself, bound only by his own conscience; from which it must follow that neither authority nor obedience ought to be taken for granted. If my father, my priest, or my king wants to exert authority over me, if he wants to give me orders, he has to be able to explain, in a way that satisfies my reason, on what grounds he must command and I must obey.

This is not the place to go into the natural and supernatural sources of authority within the family and the Church. But whence comes authority in civil and political society? It is extraordinarily important to know this. For even the priest, collecting his tithes or building his church, can do so only under the sway of the civil power. You cannot marry or bring children into the world or educate them without conforming to the laws of the state. Neither the owner of a factory nor the president of a club nor the headquarters of a union can exercise the least authority except within the legal framework determined by the government. You can neither buy a newspaper, nor take a tram, nor live in your house, nor beat your wife (or your husband), nor baptize your children unless the law ratifies your action and weighs its import.

What, then, is the source of the astonishingly universal law that gives so much power to our political leaders? The question engrossed the first philosophers thousands of years ago, and it is still a question.

Some take the easy way out by reiterating that authority comes from God. They omit to explain why God conferred it on a Stalin or a Hitler; or why, in our democracies, God would choose to express himself through the intermediary of electoral thugs and big campaign contributors.

According to others, authority is founded on force. To quote Pascal again, 'unable to make justice strong, we make strength just'. This explanation is inadequate too. For no man or group of men can impose authority on a population against its will. When injustice reaches a certain point, even soldiers and policemen refuse to obey —as witness the French, Russian, Chinese, Indo-Chinese, and other revolutions.

Still others invoke natural law, affirming that authority rests on the nature of things. Like the divine explanation, this is an abstraction; while it is not false, it fails to explain the contradictory variety of forms of authority and law. In certain societies it is the grandfather who rules, in others it is the mother, in still others the queen's eldest son. Slavery is illegal here; elsewhere it is allowed. One country sanctions divorce, another forbids it altogether. Two years ago the Padlock Law[1] governed us in Quebec, today we are free of it. 'The nature of things', then, is no great help in explaining how it is that Maurice can give orders to Pierre, and why something permitted here is forbidden elsewhere.

We must keep on looking, then. . . .

---

[1] In 1956 Frank Scott had successfully challenged the Padlock Law before the Supreme Court. This law had been passed by the government of Quebec in 1937. On the pretext of preventing the incursion of Communism into Quebec, Duplessis had given himself the discretionary power to padlock premises used by organizations alleged to be 'communist'.

3 To prevent sedition . . .

It is dangerous to tell the people that the laws are unjust;
for they obey them only because they think them just.
That is why they must be told at the same time that they
must obey them because they are laws; just as they must
obey superiors, not because they are just, but because
they are superiors. In this way all sedition is prevented.

PASCAL

I have already shown that it is not enough to appeal to
God or nature, fear or force, to explain the authority pos-
sessed by certain leaders and certain laws over the mass
of people.

Some philosophers have tried to explain this authority
by a kind of contract among the members of society,
delegating authority to some of them. This notion has its
attraction, bringing into our inquiry as it does the idea of
consent: A has authority over B because B agrees to it.
The obvious difficulty is that such a contract is an abstract idea, never having in fact been signed. In reality,
man is born into society without having been consulted,
and he has very little choice but to go on living in it.

Let us see, then, where our discussion has led us. On
the one hand we say that all men are brothers, that is to
say equals. But on the other hand wherever we look, in

whatever country we may be, we see that the great majority are subject to a small number of superiors who make the law for them. As Rousseau said, 'Man is born free, yet everywhere he is in chains. . . . How did this change come about?'

To reconcile these contradictions and unravel our difficulties, we must begin by observing that society is a given fact for man. We cannot know if there has ever existed, or will ever exist, a species of man who does not live in society but courses the woods like a lone wolf. What we do see is that wherever men live they in fact live in society and depend on a social order. Not even the criminal can escape this order, for his ignorance of the criminal code and his dislike of prison do not prevent his subjection to those institutions. The nomad, the hermit, and the gypsy also depend on the social order on whose fringes they think they live; for there is no territory in the world that does not fall under the dominion of some sovereign power. The hermit's cave, whether he likes it or not, is regulated by the laws of possession and property. The gypsy cannot tell your fortune without liability under the law of contract. And I have watched the nomads of the Asiatic steppe being required to pay duty to the Afghan treasury when their migrations took them into the Khyber Pass.

The human being, then, lives in the framework of society; and life in society cannot be pictured without subjection to an established order—that is, a government. It is in this sense that one can say that authority, philosophically speaking, comes from God or from the nature of things, since God has created man with a nature that compels him to live in society: subject, that is, to politics. Political authority comes from God in the same sense as the queen's authority in a beehive comes from God.

But we are not bees, nor are we ants, and that is why this answer by itself is not enough. Men stay free because *no one* is fully vested by God or nature with authority to rule his fellows. James I of England wrote big books to prove that he was king by divine right; he believed that his son Charles I could be too, but that did not prevent the English from cutting off his head. Louis XVI of France and Tsar Nicholas II of Russia ended their careers in much the same manner. And in democracies political parties and prime ministers that thought themselves eternal have been sent packing by the people, and will be again.

Human societies, then, differ from the beehives in that men are always free to decide what form of authority they will adopt, and who will exercise it. And it really is men who have the responsibility of taking these decisions —not God, Providence, or Nature. In the last analysis any given political authority exists only because men consent to obey it. In this sense what exists is not so much the authority as the obedience.

4 The just man must go to prison . . .

Under a government which imprisons any unjustly, the true place for a just man is also a prison . . . —the only house in a slave state in which a free man can abide with honour. THOREAU

We have seen that political authority exists only so far as men want to obey. One can therefore say that the power of governments rests on a psychological disposition on most people's part to believe that it is *good* to obey and *bad* to disobey.

Why is this belief so universal? Partly because the majority seek only their own comfort and pleasure: when these ends are assured, they ask no more than to conform to a given social order and to obey political masters who work to maintain that order. Few men are aroused by an injustice when they are sure of not being its victims themselves. That is why the newspaper *Vrai* has so much trouble in convincing people that Coffin was the victim of a judicial murder; or that a poor devil of an orphan ought to be let out of Bordeaux jail where he has languished *without trial* for eleven months.

Also, the multitude's psychological disposition to obey

is fostered by all who exercise authority in any form—
for these have a strong sense of their mutual interdepen-
dence. In the family, in the school, in the parish, or at
work, blind obedience is preached as a virtue: in this way
one can be confident of bringing up a good little people
that will cause no trouble.

As long as authority does not pass all bounds of stupidity and incompetence it is sure to hold its position. Mr
Duplessis, for instance, constantly teaches us that we
must not criticize the authority he exercises: firstly because this authority comes from God, and secondly
because he rules in the name of the Province and the
'race', values that none but a perverse spirit could assail.
Thus, a few weeks ago, our prime minister declared that
the powers given to the provincial supreme court were
not to be criticized because the former chief justice of
that court was the father of the Archbishop of Quebec,
Mgr Roy!

In saying this Mr Duplessis was trying to prove to us
that all authority is interconnected and indivisible. The
blessing of bridges, hospitals, and universities, accom-
panied by great political demonstrations, is based on a
similar piece of trickery.

We see then that governments and the majority of
the governed concur in decreeing the immutability of the
established order. It remains true, however, that most of
the authorities claiming divine right, and most of the
laws called natural, are the artificial products of education. Men believe that it is good to obey such people and
such laws because these men were born and brought up
in a civilization in which they were taught that it was
natural.

In the civilization next door, though, men obey utterly
different laws, believing just as strongly that this is good
and true and natural. 'Truth on this side of the Pyrenees,'

said Pascal, 'error on the other.' And he recognized clearly
that the surest way of provoking rebellion was to make
people think about the injustice of established laws and
customs. 'The art of opposition and revolution is to upset
established customs, tracing them to their source to point
out their lack of authority and justice.'

There is nothing wrong with doing this; on the contrary, it is often the only way to re-establish justice and
liberty among men. For society is made for man; if it
serves him badly he is entitled to overthrow it. The purpose of living in society is that every man may fulfil himself as far as possible. Authority has no justification
except to allow the establishment and development of a
system that encourages such fulfilment.

It follows that when authority in any form bullies a
man unfairly, all other men are guilty; for it is their tacit
assent that allows authority to commit the abuse. If they
withdrew their consent, authority would collapse.

That is why Thoreau believed that a just man, as proof
of solidarity with those whom he cannot defend in any
other way, must share their penalty when he thinks them
unjustly condemned. Were there not unconscious disci-
ples of Thoreau among the people who helped Jacques
Hébert pay his recent fine?[1] . . .

---

[1] On 15 February 1958 Mr Justice Wilfrid Lazure found Jacques
Hébert guilty of contempt of court, following the appearance of an
article criticizing two court decisions. The author was condemned
to three months in prison or a fine of $300–a sum which was
spontaneously contributed by the readers of *Vrai*.

5 Must the tyrant be assassinated?

When the government is illegitimate and tyrannical, each individual may destroy it by violence. . . . The tyrant makes (unjust) war on each individual; each one has the right to kill him. CANON FERNAND BOILLAT (1945)

Personally I dislike violence. And I shall have occasion later on to show that assassination is a very weak political instrument.

But how do we explain that eminent theologians—among them certain Jesuits, armed with their *imprimatur* and their *nihil obstat*—have brought themselves to teach that the social doctrine of the Church makes political assassination legitimate and even obligatory?

Our discussion so far has established that any political authority exists only because the citizens agree to obey it. This agreement, then, is the guarantee of all social order.

Now, this agreement—or 'psychological disposition to obey', as we have called it with rather more precision—is accorded only so long as the citizens find welfare and profit in it. If the people feel themselves oppressed, appeals to vague and abstract notions of general welfare, established order, and respect for authority will not in practice compel obedience. The people obey because it is easier to do so and because they are accustomed to it; this custom will be broken if the people, feeling themselves oppressed, start thinking about the possibility of suppressing the oppressors.

Tyrants always claim that their social order is founded on the common weal, the welfare of the race; but they reserve the right to define this welfare themselves, and their laws require the citizens to act accordingly. Now to credit one or several leaders with superior knowledge of what particular set of actions is best for everyone is to call in question the very basis of social morality. For the only good action, of real moral value, is a voluntary action, chosen by the enlightened thinking of the person who performs it.

It is the duty of citizens, therefore, to examine their consciences on the quality of the social order they share and the political authority they acknowledge. If the order is rotten and the authority vicious, the duty of the citizen is to obey his conscience in preference to that authority. And if the only sure way of reconstituting a just social order is to stage a revolution *against tyrannical and illegal authority*—well, then, it must be done.

So when you teach the people to obey authority, you ought to add that it is possible to disobey it with an equally good conscience. If you did so you would find, on the one hand, that the rulers would grow rather more respectful towards the governed; on the other, that the latter would become more sensitive to the notions of liberty and justice.

It follows from all this that no government, no particular régime, has an absolute right to exist. This is not a matter of divine right, natural law, or social contract: a government is an organization whose job is to fulfil the needs of the men and women, grouped in society, who consent to obey it. Consequently the value of a government derives not from the promises it makes, from what it claims to be, or from what it alleges it is defending, but from what it achieves in practice. And it is for each citizen to judge of that.

But by what standards will he form his judgement? In a society of egoists, clearly, every citizen will want a government that will cater to him personally even at the expense of others: he will therefore pledge his loyalty to a government that will give him, as circumstances require, a bottle of beer, a refrigerator, a church pavement, or a university subsidy.

But a society of egoists quickly becomes a society of slaves; for no man by himself is capable of overturning an established government. Such a government is not weakened at all when one discontented citizen refuses to obey the authorities, for they simply put him in prison.

To remain free, then, citizens must seek their welfare in a social order that is just to the largest number; in practice only the majority has the power to make and unmake governments. It follows that men can live free and at peace only if their society is just.

6 Obedience— but to whom?

*Like the apostles, I would rather obey God than men . . .
I condemn these newspapers, and like the Bishop of Prato
I am ready to be dragged through the courts rather than
be silent.'* CARDINAL LÉGER (9 MARCH 1958)

I was saying last week that in some circumstances—if,
for instance, a social order is rotten, tyrannical, illegal,
and vicious—it may be the duty of the citizens to obey
their consciences rather than political authority. And now
here are Cardinal Léger and the Bishop of Prato saying
the same thing: they will obey their own truth, even if it
conflicts with the law of the land.

Such a doctrine must obviously be applied prudently
and circumspectly or we shall have anarchy. One citizen
will refuse conscription because he conscientiously believes that war is evil. Another will defraud the treasury
because he thinks taxes are too high and undermine the
family. A third will ignore the closing hours of bars, or
the speed limit, because he thinks these laws antiquated
and out of date. In this way, with everyone arrogating to
himself the right to judge each law that inconveniences
him, sooner or later everyone will be living in a state of
constant lawless disorder; eventually strength, audacity,
and guile will usurp the place of law, and the life of man

will be, in the words of Hobbes, 'solitary, poor, nasty, brutish, and short'.

So, even though it is the duty of citizens to make conscientious judgements on the value of laws and the integrity of rulers, it would be a mistake to conclude that every citizen is automatically entitled to break the laws and get rid of the leaders he dislikes. Assassination of tyrants, though authorized by Canon Boillat of Saint-Maurice Abbey, and civil disobedience, though invoked this week by His Eminence Cardinal Léger, are clearly exceptional measures, to be undertaken only as a last resort against illegitimate and tyrannical governments.

And it is precisely to avoid the necessity of such violence and disorder that most civilized peoples provide mechanisms whereby citizens can fight against laws they disapprove of without going outside the law or becoming conscientious objectors or political martyrs.

I shall have occasion in ensuing articles to show that among these mechanisms democracy seems the most effective as well as the most consistent with peace, justice, and liberty. But today I shall content myself with giving one example of a protest mounted peacefully and lawfully against a social order, and laws, conscientiously judged to be bad.

Last week the students of the six Quebec universities decided to boycott their lectures for a day. And there was no lack of rectors, deans, and professors to denounce the gesture with talk of Bolshevism, to contrive penalties, and to utter threats. Two institutions, one of them religious, went back on their word after having consented to rent halls to the students. In contrast, there were other university authorities who showed sympathy for the students.

Now, what was this all about? For the last few years,

trade unions, teachers' associations, royal commissions, chambers of commerce, national organizations, and conferences of educators had been denouncing our present educational system as inadequate and backward. Almost alone among free men, the students kept quiet.

But at last, understanding that they owed a heavy debt to a society that feeds, clothes, and shelters them during the long unproductive period of their education, grasping their obligation to the social classes that toil so that they may consume, perceiving that for these reasons education should in fairness be accessible to all classes and talent should be the only criterion for admission to all levels of instruction, the students drew up a memorandum calling for the democratization of the system and for free education.

It was then that the political authorities refused to receive the students. For the latter not to have reacted would have been to behave like slaves. For it was intolerable that a head of government should be able to dismiss as unimportant a reform demanded by a large section of the enlightened public; as I said last week, it is intolerable that one man should claim to know better than the majority what kind of social and political order is *good* for them.

It is not a question of the value or the effectiveness of the boycott itself. The point is that this gesture had been decided on democratically by the students themselves. That some of them chose not to vote clearly has nothing to do with the case: they were implicitly endorsing whatever decision the majority should take. After all, if elections could be invalidated by large abstentions, neither Mr Diefenbaker nor Mr Duplessis nor Mr Fournier[1] would hold power legally.

So the students' boycott is worth reflecting on; some

---

[1] Mr Sarto Fournier was mayor of Montreal at the time.

young citizens showed their elders that there were ways
of judging a social order conscientiously, and condemning it, without disturbing the peace or breaking the law.
For it would not be unlawful for the students to decide
not to go to lectures that they had already paid for;
otherwise, Mr Duplessis would have to be charged each
time he bought bus tickets—and decided to walk instead.

7 Undermining the majesty of the state

The chief end of society is to allow its members, collectively and individually, to live a full life. ARISTOTLE

A mistaken attitude is implanted among us whereby the state is regarded as a remote and capricious master, to be approached fearfully and submissively. This master may be of service to society, of course, but it is better to ask as little of him as possible; with such a tyrant, family life and religious faith are never secure.

There is, of course, a historical explanation for this attitude: under the French régime the state did indeed appear as a remote and authoritarian master, whereas under the British it was for many years inimical to our ethnic group.

It is true that since 1867—and emphatically since 1931 —the state has been for all practical purposes in the hands of those whom we choose from election to election. But our perverse attitude remains. And our conception of the state as a taloned ogre, from whom citizens must forcibly wrest their meagre liberties, has had unfortunate effects on us. This is the source of our bad citizenship and political immorality; having learned to distrust the state as an enemy, citizens feel no guilt at making secret war on it. The same people who virtuously preach respect for authority falsify their tax returns, smuggle, cheerfully evade the law, and bribe public figures.

At the same time we are used to identifying with the concept of the state all kinds of power that we dread: imperialism, statism, Freemasonry, Communism, atheism, and so on. For fear of being led to our eternal damnation by these evils, we have prevented the state from doing anything to increase its power, so that as a people we are helpless to take collective action to solve our collective problems—economic weakness, backward education, public health, and housing; and so on . . .

Yet we live in society precisely so that we *can* tackle collectively the problems that we cannot solve individually.

When the day came that neither the individual nor private enterprise could provide the bridges and roads needed for travel, organize the police and fire brigades required for public safety, or devise the water and sewage systems necessary for hygiene, the community simply decided to solve these problems communally, through the state. And nobody dreamt of crying 'Communism!'

Now, what the state could do for sewers, could it not do in other realms where individuals by themselves cannot provide the answer? If the state can organize a fire brigade to protect our goods, why can it not organize a teaching brigade to develop our minds, or knock down slums to protect our way of life?

After all, as Aristotle said, men live in society so that they can live a full life. The point of human society is that men living together, by mutual help, co-operation, and the division of labour, can fulfil themselves better than if they lived apart. If men could not direct their collective effort to that end, they might as well go off and live all alone in the woods and on the hills.

And the state is by definition the instrument whereby human society collectively organizes and expresses itself. A sovereign society that fears the state is a moribund society, unconvinced of the usefulness of its own existence as a group.

Will anyone think I am preaching statism? On the contrary, I am preaching the doctrine of the servant state. For if I say today that the state should do more in the name of the community it is only after repeatedly saying in my six earlier essays that no political authority has an unconditional right to exist. I want the state to do more, but only after we have stopped thinking of it as an absolute master. In fact, if we were to extend the powers of the state without having multiplied our means of controlling its policy and limiting its methods of acting, we would tend to increase our enslavement. That is why I am wary of those who preach indiscriminate nationalization without setting themselves first to undermine the undue majesty of political power.

8 The election

It is therefore a complete error . . . to claim that authority does not belong to those who exercise it, but that they hold it only by virtue of a mere mandate that can be recalled by the people at any time. SCRIPT READ ON 'MORNING PRAYER—MORNING DEVOTIONS', CBC (20 JUNE 1956)

On the morning of the last provincial election a script was read over CBF on 'the source of power', a fragment of which is quoted above.

To have broadcast such a statement seems to me inopportune and ill-timed—I would even call it immoral, if it were not for the somewhat restricted meaning that adjective has acquired among us. On the very day the people are going to vote, the one day they can conscientiously and effectively voice their judgement on the men and the laws they have obeyed for four years—it it not scandalous that this day should be chosen to tell them authoritatively that *authority belongs to those who exercise it?*

If, on the very day of the election, the people cannot recall the mandate of the politicians in office, it follows that the people have no right to vote against the government. Here, surely, is a partial explanation of the high proportion of abstentions in our elections. For, if every vote not cast for the government party is a sin, many people will choose not to vote at all.

And as for those who do vote, why should they take

it seriously? Since authority belongs to those who exercise it, and (as this same 'Morning Prayer' also said) 'all this talk of the origin, the basis, and the structure of this so-called [sic!] sovereignty of the people is purely arbitrary'—since, in short, the people have nothing to do with the matter, why not enjoy yourself on election day, go and have a quick one while these fake protests are going on, and sell your vote to the highest bidder as your vote is meaningless anyway? No wonder the magistrates acquit electoral thugs and give them back their 'working tools'—as actually happened in Montreal.[1]

It is utterly useless to preach electoral morality to a people while minimizing or ridiculing the idea of popular sovereignty. You might as well preach Christian morality after ridiculing Christ. And as a matter of fact that is just what has been happening in our society for a long time. On the Sunday before the election the priest reads us the appendix to the Roman ritual so as to put us on our guard against excess on voting day. But why does he not also talk to us about the role of the people in the granting of authority?

Some open-minded clergymen do denounce political thuggery; but very few indeed take as much trouble to correct the errors and counter the anti-democratic tendencies of our traditional social philosophy. High-minded men, devoted to the public good, will organize in the hope of restoring some reason and wholesomeness to our public administration. But how many of them ever dream of basing their movement ultimately on a really democratic philosophy and structure, allowing the members to choose their leaders, debate the program, and so on?

---

[1] The reference is to those whom some supporters of the Union Nationale called 'honest workers', and whose 'working tools' proved to be baseball bats which they used on political opponents during the provincial and some municipal elections.

To sum up, I am amazed that so many worthy people preach the morality of democracy without first preaching its doctrine. It seems to me that they are wasting their time. Furthermore, I would be wary of a wave of political morality unaccompanied by a wind of true democracy—that is the way of fascism.

But we will have to discuss the state and its functions before our political 'approaches' lead us up to the plateau of democracy. If I have glanced at it this week it is just because we are going through a general election,[2] and that is an excellent opportunity to remind voters that authority is *not* the property of those who exercise it.

---

[2] In the federal election of April 1958, the minority government of John G. Diefenbaker that had taken office in 1957 achieved a phenomenal landslide, winning 208 seats.

9 A state made to measure

How many worthy souls look on the state as a super-natural power to be propitiated rather than as the repository of the will of the people? The sins of government seem to them as inevitable as thunder or flood: faced with such natural phenomena, the wise man submits to the inevitable. ANDRÉ LAURENDEAU

Two weeks ago, while Mr Laurendeau[1] was publishing these lines, I was describing here the pernicious consequences of our mental habit of thinking of the state as an ogre.

This attitude is mistaken. It is not true: the state is neither a supernatural power that unleashes irresistible plagues upon us nor an ogre that gobbles up families and crucifixes.

In any stable, self-governing society, the state is simply a creature, emanating from the members of that society. In other words, the state is precisely what the people want it to be, and has only such reality as they choose to give it. Its authority is limited by the general agreement to obey it. And it can exert only as much force as the citizens lend it.

That is why I cannot agree with *Le Devoir* of 17

[1] Editor of *Le Devoir*; later, until his death in 1968, co-chairman of the Royal Commission on Bilingualism and Biculturalism.

October 1956, which said: 'Liberty is not a free gift, but a conquest. There is no liberty but what is wrested from authority.' This made Mr Léopold Richer[2] very nervous, too. He wrote at once: 'Did you read it? Did you really understand it? This is insubordination to all established authority, religious or civil. This is sedition. This is rebellion. Gérard Filion has descended to preaching revolution.' And so on . . .

Well! We are still waiting to glimpse the red rays of sedition, rebellion, and revolution—no doubt because Mr Richer is vigilant, because *Ici-Montréal* (8 March) is displaying 'pin-ups' in defence of the Pope, and because *Nouvelles et Potins* (19 October) rallies to the aid of the Jesuits against the distortions of hypocrites and pseudo-intellectuals.

But what is more serious is that the decent people have not yet 'conquered' their liberty. (Ask Mr DesMarais, the late chairman of the Metropolitan Commission.[3] Ask the miners of Murdochville.[4] And have a word with three students[5] who have taken up residence in the provincial parliament building.) Now, if we are not making better progress, may it not be that we are defining the problem wrongly when we speak of liberty as a conquest?

Liberty *is* a free gift—a birthright, which distinguishes

[2] Editor of *Notre-Temps*.

[3] The 'DesMarais Bill', requiring candidates for the mayoralty of Montreal to have resided in the city for three years, was so called from its evident intention of forestalling the candidacy of Mr Des-Marais, who lived in the suburb of Outremont.

[4] Murdochville, in the copper-mining country of the Gaspé peninsula, had been the scene of a major strike in 1957.

[5] In 1958 Prime Minister Duplessis had refused the request of the presidents of the six Quebec universities for an interview. Before the refusal arrived, the presidents delegated three students to go to the legislative assembly and wait until the prime minister would receive them. These three students, Francine Laurendeau, Jean-Pierre Goyer, and Bruno Meloche, cooled their heels in the parliamentary corridors from 7 March until early May.

man from beast. To allow human society to develop in order and justice, men agree to some restrictions on their liberty, and obey the authority of the state. In consequence, the game of politics should consist less in wresting liberties from a grudging state than in grudgingly delegating powers to the state.

Citizens must take care, then, to delegate to it no more authority, no more force, than are strictly necessary to establish a just social order, protect that order from harm, and make sure that it will progress. In these conditions the stability of the state will depend on its governing in such a way as to assure the unfailing loyalty of the citizenry. In other words the state cannot and must not make laws that do not tally by and large with what the citizens want; if it does, they will defy its laws, until the time comes to overthrow it. The real purpose of laws, then, is to educate the citizen in the common good, and persuade him to behave in the public interest, rather than to command and constrain.

It is right to say, then, that the state is an article made to measure by its citizens, according to the precise amount of obedience they are prepared to offer it. The moment a state, grown too powerful, too weak, or too misguided, ceases to make the citizens feel they are governed justly, they have the right to insist on a change —peacefully if they possess the means, by force if they do not.

We shall see later that the merit of democracy is precisely that it makes peaceful changes possible.

10 Tyrannicide, the Jesuits, and Father de Léry

It is one thing to show a man that he is in an error, and another to put him in possession of truth. JOHN LOCKE

Certain men of learning have done me the honour of commenting on these essays. The comments are hostile, but what does that matter? Political discussion on the theoretical level is so rare in French Canada that any step in that direction is a step forward.

Father de Léry's article in *Relations* (April 1958) is especially welcome. He knows his subject, and he shows us that according to Catholic doctrine any patriot at all may assassinate an unjust and illegitimate tyrant. The case of a tyrant who oppresses his subjects, but did obtain power legitimately, is more complicated: only the 'representatives of the people' can decree his death and arrange for his assassination.

The question of deciding who the 'representatives of the people' are is a bit tricky, clearly. Father de Léry refrains from tackling it, unfortunately; and I must leave it to the theologians to sort out their little problem. For my part I am concerned only with the doctrine as a whole. At the beginning of the article under arraignment,

I wrote that I disliked violence. Since it seems necessary
to dot my i's, let me add that it repels me. That is precisely why, throughout this series, I am trying to raise
politics to the level of conscience, and am preaching a
political philosophy directed towards democracy and the
obsolescence of the theologies of political assassination.

That is clear enough, isn't it? What is less clear is what
is bothering Father de Léry. He complains that 'three
lines [by Trudeau] sufficed to incriminate eminent theologians, among them certain Jesuits. . . . We will need
nearly a page to re-establish the facts.'

Now I incriminated nobody. There were no facts to
re-establish, as is proved by the fact that Father de Léry
recites in detail the theology of tyrannicide to which I
made only a passing allusion, quoting Canon Boillat—
who expounds exactly the same doctrine as Father de
Léry. My purpose became quite clear in the rest of the
article: to establish that 'it is the duty of citizens . . .
to examine their consciences on the quality of the
social order they share and the political authority they
acknowledge'.

I am sorry that such a brief foray into theology was
enough to trouble the consciences of the Jesuits of *Relations*. True, I was thinking of Mariana[1] when I wrote the
essay, but I was also thinking of Suarez[2] and of the great
Cardinal Bellarmine, who did so much to establish a
distinction between the spiritual and the temporal with
regard to the authority of the clergy. And I was thinking
just as much of their remote predecessors, of the theolo-

---

[1] Juan de Mariana (1536-1624), Spanish Jesuit whose thesis that it
was lawful to overthrow a tyrant contributed greatly to the suspicion with which Jesuits were regarded, especially after the
assassination of Henry IV in 1610.

[2] Francisco Suarez (1548-1617), Spanish Jesuit who denied the
divine right of kings; James I of England had one of his books
burned by the common hangman.

gians, like William of Occam, who laid the foundation of the theories that made it possible to set bounds to the despotism of princes. In short, some theologians (not excluding certain Jesuits) have played a leading role in the evolution of political thought, and it is partly thanks to them that the liberty of the citizen has managed to prevail over the absolutism of kings. Merely because, at certain periods, they have had to consider the theory of assassination is no reason for them to have a guilty conscience today.

But Father de Léry seems perfectly well aware of these matters, and if left to himself would certainly have felt no call to blush for the Jesuit Mariana, whose book 'was many times republished *by the Protestants*'. (The italics are *Relations'*s.) It follows that Father de Léry's article was written under orders, as sometimes happens among the Jesuits. Somebody must have told him that Trudeau was a malcontent and that his articles were considered to have a Protestant tendency. Hence the tone of refutation that the good father felt obliged to adopt in writing, in effect, the same thing I did!

The pity of all this is that neither you nor I found out what Father de Léry thought about democracy, or about the theory of legal sovereignty that I outlined in my articles. *Relations* has before now been able to take up the cudgels most effectively against the political immorality of our society; but might not my remarks of two weeks back have some application to that magazine? 'It is utterly useless to preach electoral morality to a people while minimizing or ridiculing the idea of popular sovereignty.'

Commentaries on the history of theology have their place, certainly, in a magazine like *Relations*. But if that magazine is ever again tempted to do me the honour of commenting on my *Vrai* articles, I venture to hope that it might be to touch on some of their more important aspects. As for the criticism of a prudent friend, which Father de Léry recommends to me at the end of his article, I should like it to be offered by someone who would not hesitate to depart a little from the vocabulary of an instructor in 'Philosophy II' speaking of democracy and concluding that monarchy is the only perfect form of government.

11 The revolution and Mr André Dagenais

The surest way to prevent seditions (if the times do bear it) is to take away the matter of them.   FRANCIS BACON

The front page of the weekly *Salaberry* of 13 March last bore two headlines, each running its full width:

TEAR DOWN THE TAVERNS

AVERT THE REVOLUTION

Thus did Mr André Dagenais, the editor, announce his political program for the week. If I am correctly informed, he has been more successful with the second plank of his platform than with the first. Although it was in connection with the second that I got involved, it would be premature to conclude that Mr Dagenais's ideas have triumphed over mine.

On page 3 we learn that Mr Dagenais only wants 'to avert the *bad* revolution', i.e. mine. As for the good revolution (his), the revolution of the 'organic City' and the 'basic triad', he wants us to plunge head first into it. That is his own business, obviously, and I shall leave him to sort it out with the police. But for my part—must I repeat it yet again?—I am against revolution. That is why, following Bacon's advice, I am trying to 'take away the matter' of it. For more than two months I have been preaching here the gospel of democracy, precisely because it is a system of government that allows changes *without* revolution, *without* illegality. As long as we have freedom of speech and free elections, I think it childish and irresponsible to want to drag us out of our political ills by violence.

Mr Dagenais finds that my text is not distinguished by strict logic and he may well be right. But how can he suppose that this weakness is deliberately adopted in order to 'provoke the theologians to reply'? To judge by the *Salaberry*, Mr Dagenais ought to know that one does not write for a weekly with the same strict care as for a magazine or a book. He is not strictly serving logic, nor even his own honour, when he voices the unfounded suspicion that I want to baffle the theologians and even to 'dethrone God, Lawgiver of cities, in order to worship popular consensus'.

The baselessness of Mr Dagenais's suspicions becomes clear if one considers how he chops up my text and reinterprets it. Notice his method in the following passage: 'The title of the latest article was "Must the Tyrant be Assassinated?" In the dream pursued by Mr Trudeau, the tyrant—make no mistake about it—is the Hon. Maurice Duplessis! This is a stupid thing to say.' Stupid indeed, like many other things Mr Dagenais says; but it is important to take note that it is Mr Dagenais who says them. As for me, I specifically said in the first sentence of the article under arraignment that I was against violence.

In another place Mr Dagenais taxes me with Rousseauism because I quote Rousseau's well-known phrase 'Man is born free'. It is as if I were to accuse my parish priest of pederasty because, like André Gide, he says that God is everywhere! I have quoted Rousseau, as I have quoted Plato, Aristotle, Pascal, and Locke, because they have all played important parts, kindly note, in the evolution of political thought. But, to tell the truth, I knew when I quoted even the most inoffensive phrase of Rousseau's that I was setting a snare for all the watchdogs of reaction. I might have known that I would find Mr Dagenais in it, on all fours along with Léopold Richer.

Mr Dagenais discusses the text in much the same manner as Mr Richer. From a series of articles he selects the sentences that are most upsetting to his own rigidified categories of thought and, without pausing to consider whether they might be true or even worth discussing, he puts them end to end, trundles them along to the civil and religious authorities, and says: 'Look at this! Listen to that! This man is going to end up in jail, or excommunicated.' And, having thus denounced me, he rests his case.

Except that there is still the argument from authority. Mr Dagenais throws in my face a text from Leo XIII condemning a certain form of democracy. And what if I were to answer that Pius XII approved of another form of democracy, and that that is the one I am advocating? Mr Dagenais would reply that the doctrine of popular sovereignty was condemned. And I would retort that so was liberalism, so was Galileo, and so was St Thomas Aquinas —three times over. These old clichés!

I find this style of discussion petty. I leave to the Church as teacher the job of taking care of orthodoxy, and I am sure it needs no help in this from Mr Dagenais. For my part I am setting forth here certain political and legal theories, not a theology. If on occasion my concepts or my phraseology differ from traditional teachings, it may possibly be because those teachings are a few centuries out of date. In any case this ought to be open to discussion in the context of political and legal science.

If we may say that in a monarchy the king is sovereign,

why should one not hold that in a parliamentary democracy Parliament is sovereign—that when a republic is being formed the constituent assembly is sovereign—that at certain times of direct democracy sovereignty resides in the people?

Over the centuries that separate Jean Bodin from John Austin, the legal notion of sovereignty has been developed and enriched. All writers have not always been in agreement—far from it; but at each step it has been only the ignorant or the stoolpigeons for whom the debate began and ended with the single argument from authority.

12 Social contract and popular sovereignty

The people puts a man in authority so that he will rule justly, rendering to each his due. . . . If, then, this man breaks the contract according to the terms whereby he was chosen, creating disorder in the heart of those things he was supposed to put in order, reason requires that the people should be released from obedience. MANEGOLD OF LAUTENBACH[1]

At the beginning of this series of articles I proposed to the reader to reflect in simple terms on the forms and limits of political authority. In a province where the democratic reflexes are neither frequent nor deepseated, I thought a popular weekly could usefully teach the extent of the responsibility borne by the citizens in the choice and supervision of their leaders.

To this end I have sketched out here a theory of obedience, certain minor aspects of which have some originality, I admit; but on the whole my approaches have

---

[1] A twelfth-century monk who wrote tracts supporting the papal against the imperial power.

followed in tracks as old as political philosophy itself, paths trodden by thinkers of all countries and all periods: pagans and Christians, Protestants and Catholics, fathers of the Church and monks, laity and clergy, Dominicans and Franciscans, royalists and republicans, anti-monarchists and legitimists, parliamentarians and Levellers.

But for well-informed Quebeckers, apparently, none of these people have ever existed; the history of political thought begins with Mgr Paquet! It is not surprising, then, that two weeks ago I had to interrupt the normal course of these approaches to assure the Jesuits of *Relations* that my theories were not Protestant, and to avow to the theologians of the *Salaberry* and *Notre-Temps* that I had never questioned any Catholic dogma. Today I am forced to contradict a worthy, well-accredited (and very pretty) lady who is whispering in the salons that my theories make me a Communist!

Let everyone be reassured—and instructed. Neither the Protestants, nor Jean-Jacques Rousseau, nor le Sillon, nor Karl Marx are the inventors or exclusive proprietors of the philosophy of political consensus expounded in the present series of articles and often embodied in systems of social contract or popular sovereignty.

On the contrary, the founders of Protestantism rejected these theories; Luther, Tyndale, and Calvin all defended the absolute power of the Prince, and the first could write: 'It is improper for anyone calling himself a Christian to oppose his government, whether it is just or unjust. . . . Disobedience is a worse sin than murder, impurity, theft. . . .' That is as strong as Paul's Epistle to the Romans. It was only with the Counter-Reformation that the Protestants began to adopt social-contract theories.

But these theories go back to the very origins of political thought. Traces of it are found in Plato, in

Epicurus, in the *lex regia* of the Romans, and in Cicero, for whom the authority of the state flows from the collective power of the people. The doctrine of the Contract of Government was completely accepted in the Middle Ages, especially at the time of the War of the Investitures (see the quotation from Manegold above). But in its modern form the doctrine of the contract was expressed for the first time (O irony of nomenclature!) by Duplessis-Mornay, the presumed author of *Vindiciae contra tyrannos*. After this Huguenot there were three Jesuits who were inspired by the contract theory: Bellarmine in Italy, Suarez in Spain, and Parsons in England—who used it against Elizabeth. In the seventeenth century, contract theoreticians swarmed: Althusius, Grotius, Pufendorf, Selden, Parker, Milton, Prynne and Lilburne, then finally Spinoza, Hobbes, and Locke. The doctrine likewise appeared in the United States with Paine and Jefferson, and then at last in France with Rousseau; it remains to mention Germany with Kant and Fichte.

Theories of popular sovereignty are even more widespread, if possible. Let us just recall precursors like St Isidore, and tyrannicides like the monk John of Salisbury and the Jesuit Mariana. The idea that political authority flows from the will of the governed has deep foundations in medieval theology. Thus, with John of Paris, *'populo faciente et Deo inspirante'*; Marsilius of Padua and St Thomas Aquinas also hold that God is only the *'causa remota'* of authority; William of Occam sees *'imperium a Deo et tamen per homines'*; and for Nicolas of Cusa the chief of state is *'quasi in se omnium voluntatem gestans'*. Next will come the Jesuits who, in order to deny the transcendental origin of the state, will be almost unanimous in affirming the doctrine of the original sovereignty of the people: Suarez especially, but also Molina, Schmier, Victoria, and Vasquez.

Once more: I make no claim that all these thinkers developed identical systems of thought—far from it; but it is to the credit of them all that they elaborated systems that, by invoking some sort of popular participation or consent, set limits to political authority, protected the liberty of the citizens, and assured the full development of the individual. Why am I reproached for tending, much more modestly, towards the same ends? Is it thought that liberty is not at stake here? Or is liberty not thought worth preserving?

But will I be allowed to stop there? Are those names not enough to reassure the lay theologians who believe only the argument from authority? And are they not enough, dear madam, to convince you that Communism has nothing to do with my approaches? I hope so; for I should very much like to close the parenthesis I have kept open for two weeks, and resume my reflections on the assumption that I have a few open-minded readers left.

13 The statesman as servant

Those who possess authority in civil society . . . are in the service of those whom they govern. JOINT PASTORAL LETTER ON THE LABOUR PROBLEM (1950)

Duplessis gives to his province. ELECTION POSTER

Duplessis gives his province. ELECTION POSTER

When I spoke here a few weeks ago of undermining the undue majesty of political power, it was certainly not in the hope that we would tumble into anarchy. The state is the instrument whereby political society is organized, expresses itself, and takes collective action; the point is not to destroy it but to make it such as to serve the aims of that society adequately. In other words an exaggerated sense of the majesty of the state must not be allowed to prevent it from being a good servant. And it is in this sense that I could hope for a state made to measure.

Under these circumstances the true statesman is not one who gives orders to his fellow-citizens so much as he is one who devotes himself to their service. True, one sometimes hears it said that such a man 'serves by ruling', but that is not my view. In a constitutional society it is not men, but rather laws, that control us. The rulers are themselves subject to the laws, and they can exert authority only as far as the law allows. Our obedience, then, is not to individuals but to the general will of the nation, a will embodied in laws, to whose service and execution the rulers are appointed.

The statesman may well think differently from his fellow-citizens on certain subjects, he can try to convey his special wisdom to them; but in the final analysis it is the general will that must prevail, not his own will. That is why the statesman must be attentive to the needs of all sectors of society, with no bias towards thwarting any one of them, and must wish only to reconcile them all and direct them towards the general interest.

Thus, one can say—at a pinch—that a prime minister 'gives himself' to his country or his province, in the sense that the time he devotes to the administration of public business is out of proportion to the indemnity he receives from the public treasury. But it does not necessarily follow that such a gift is always to the advantage of the recipients: there are some gifts one would do well not to accept, as the Trojans learned to their cost some years ago!

If, however, one can tolerate it—again at a pinch—when heads of governments boast of having served the community (it rather reminds me of a bus-driver who praises himself for driving his bus), one can never tolerate it when a public man refuses to serve the community. When someone joins the civil service the least one can demand of him is that he should render service and be civil. That's what he's there for.

We should start, then, by banishing from our political *mores* the whole concept that a prime minister *gives* bridges, roads, schools to his province. These are works that society needs, that it gives to itself and pays for through taxes. A prime minister gives nothing at all (unless it is his superfluous services); quite simply, he works in the service of the state as an instrument through which *society gives to itself.*

A bad statesman, then, is one who refuses to serve the community and goes so far as to obstruct the mechanisms by which society serves itself.

Either a region needs a bridge, a road, a school, or it doesn't. If it doesn't need them, the statesman has no right to promise them. If it does need them, he has no right to refuse them. The Hon. Maurice Duplessis and the Hon. Paul Sauvé are therefore bad statesmen when they say to the voters of a constituency, 'Vote for so-and-so and we'll give you a bridge.' These servants who lay down conditions rather than doing what they are paid to do are bad servants: they ought to be fired.

When Mr Clodomir Ladouceur, member for Verchères, allows the school at Saint-Amable to be closed when he could have prevented it—as he said himself: 'If the members of the school board had come to see me, I would have arranged it for them and the government would have met the deficit without saying a word—we're not crazy!'—he is a bad servant and ought to be fired.

When a government that is upset by a short interruption in the electrical service refuses to be upset by a long interruption in the educational service, it is a bad servant and ought to be fired.

When a prime minister refuses for four months to receive the delegates of twenty-one thousand university students who politely seek an interview, he is a bad servant and ought to be fired.

We're not crazy . . .

14 The argument from authority

Prime Minister Duplessis stated that he was against the establishment of a system of free education in Quebec. He added that the Church condemns such a system.

CANADIAN PRESS DISPATCH (6 DECEMBER 1956)

Every cathedral shall be endowed with a benefice sufficient for a master who shall teach clergy and poor pupils at no charge. THIRD LATERAN COUNCIL (1179)

A look at educational questions today will allow me to develop last week's idea, namely that the statesman must serve the general will of the nation and never obstruct the mechanisms whereby society serves itself.

Now, one of the most methodical and pernicious forms of obstruction in use among us seems to me to be the argument from authority. Rather than put political questions on the rational level, where the pro and con can be discussed in logical and enlightened terms, rather than aim at a state of maturity in which free men will make their political choices responsibly and with dignity, everything possible seems to be done to save intellectual labour. 'Why think?' we seem to say. 'The question was settled long ago by the Pope or the philosopher so-and-so.' In this way, sometimes, the authority of the great dead allows a few people to lead a great life.

The politicians who invoke the argument from authority demonstrate not only the weakness of their own intellects but their contempt for the intellects of their audience. To assume thus that the people are incompetent to decide for themselves, by themselves, is to prepare the ground for dictatorship; for when the people don't make decisions there are always 'chiefs' to do it for them.

In our society such politicians have downgraded religion in the same way. Because they are speaking to a Catholic people, they resort most often to religious arguments. Thus, we were told that the religious authorities had condemned the CCF, just as our grandfathers were told they had condemned the Liberal Party; both arguments eventually turned out to be false. They told us that the Popes were against state ownership, with the result that the Ontario Hydro got fifty years' head start over Quebec. They told us that the social doctrine of the Church condemned socialistic measures; thanks to this, our aged wait ten years longer for their pension than the aged of other provinces; and a whole generation has had the advantage of growing up in the promiscuity of the slums. Christ, too, is still a useful authority for politicians who want to delay health insurance and various reforms in labour law: don't you know that the poor always ye have with you?

If I were bishop, Pope, or simple theologian, all these delays and errors perpetrated in my name would eventually make me feel rather disturbed; and for my own part I would lose some of my eagerness to encourage such practices.

The realm of education provides us with an example worth thinking about. From the earliest centuries of our history the Church has been identified with the cause of education. For a long time the scholars and philosophers of western civilization were recruited almost exclusively from the ranks of churchmen. Émile Durkheim (not a suspect witness!), writing of the beginning of the Middle Ages, says: 'If the Church had not existed at this moment, there would have been an end of humane culture, and one wonders what would have become of civilization.' Later, popes and councils—notably the eleventh Ecumenical Council—ordained free instruction for poor pupils. Later still, orders like the Brothers of the Christian Schools were founded, whose first rule laid down that they must 'maintain free schools'.

Now, what has become of these shining traditions among us? By perverting the argument from authority, the politicians have managed to identify the Church with obscurantism. For three-quarters of a century they have been telling us that the Church condemned governments that concerned themselves with education as tainted with freemasonry; to this very day the prime minister invokes the authority of the Church against free education.

In consequence we still have no ministry of education,[1] our rate of school attendance is pathetically low, and it still costs a French Canadian two hundred dollars a year more than an English Canadian to go beyond the level of elementary education.

Still worse, Catholics listen without blenching when the Minister of Youth, speaking in the name of 'the only Catholic government in North America', uses the very language of Voltaire and his friends. For in fact, when the Hon. Paul Sauvé declares that free education will just make taxi-drivers discontented with their lot and long for doctorates, he is reviving on behalf of Catholics the idiocies of the enemies of Catholicism. In 1763 La Chalotais wrote: 'The Christian teaching brothers . . . teach reading and writing to fellows who ought to be learning to draw and handle a plane and a file, and don't want to

---

[1] This ministry was not created until 13 May 1964.

any more.' And Voltaire answered: 'I thank you for rejecting study for the working class. As a landowner I ask you to provide us with labourers, not tonsured clergy.'

This curious reversal ought to make some of us reflect on the awkwardness of the argument from authority. For has it not put Voltaire, the Union Nationale, and the Church in the same camp?

15 The jitters

I would, I think, have loved liberty in any age, but in the times in which we live I feel inclined to adore it.

DE TOCQUEVILLE

I have explained in these articles the danger implicit in regarding the state as a capricious ogre. It is this distrust that has prevented French Canada from putting the state to work for the community, in realms where individuals or groups by themselves lack the means of acting: education, economic emancipation, social welfare, and so on.

It would not have been an unmitigated evil if only our mistaken and suspicious attitude had produced a healthy political liberalism among our fellow-citizens. The state would certainly not have intervened to serve the community; but neither would it have intervened to bully individuals and terrorize groups.

Nothing of the kind happened, and fear is firmly established among us. With that unfailing flair that seems to lead our people from one political abomination to another, we have freely chosen the worst of both worlds: we have done nothing to make the state serve us, but we have succeeded admirably in helping it enslave us.

We are that living absurdity—a craven people that makes itself the servant of the state; and this is the true definition of totalitarianism. I am not thinking so much of that horde of clowns and rascals, the flunkeys of politics, who live on the crumbs from the state's table. A brood like that is no direct threat to liberty; it is usually content to surrender its own without envying anybody else's. All the same, it must be added that the practice of granting favours by way of political 'protection' is debilitating to the body politic. But it is not the rascals who are to blame, it is the politicians. (Mind you, the two terms are not mutually exclusive.) For this system, besides helping to spread the slave mentality with which our population is already seriously infected, is in reality very expensive. If entry to the civil service, the police, and various government jobs were based on competence rather than 'protection', the state would gain in efficiency much more than it would lose by sending all the incompetents into retirement, to the workhouse or to school, and all the thugs to prison. But the true guilty parties are those in authority in various fields who set the example of political enslavement.

It is noticeable, for instance, that those labour leaders who are most opposed to political action on the part of the unions are generally the same ones who vie with each other in the special form of political action called lickspittling, with the object of consolidating their positions or of obtaining personal favours.

Similarly, in another field, the authorities who blame the students for forcing the state to serve the cause of education are the same ones who only succeed (by secret pilgrimages) in selling their teaching, their institutions, and their persons into slavery to the political machine. And if I were called Mgr Chartier[1]—P.D. or not—before I stated gratuitously and 'categorically that the three students had been bribed by people who wanted to make

[1] The former Vice-Rector of the University of Montreal, Mgr Émile Chartier was at this time chaplain of the federation of former pupils of the Brothers of the Sacred Heart in the ecclesiastical provinces of Sherbrooke and Arthabaska.

political capital' I would ask myself if the political brib-
ers had not come a lot closer to home than that. This
educator, who in so urgent a matter still talks of making
a complaint 'in due course', puts me in mind of Father
Marcotte,[2] who is forever expecting to find 'free education . . . laid at our doorstep'.

But the youngest among us can be equally edifying.
On a journey to Quebec last week, I learned that three
groups—the Young Agriculturists, the Playground Su-
pervisors, and the Confederation of Playgrounds and
Leisure Activities of the Province of Quebec—had suc-
cumbed to political pressure and cancelled their plans to
hold a convention at Maison Montmorency. This is a
Dominican house whose Superior[3] has too firm a belief
in liberty to be loved by our provincial government.
The province therefore blackmailed the associations
by threatening to cut off their subsidies. Result: the three
associations will hold their convention of cowards elsewhere. Moral: it's not only at the Conservatory that the
young are taught to sing.

But the coast-to-coast chicken championship is held by
the Canadian Clubs. For half a dozen years these clubs of
professional and business men had been asking Father
Georges-Henri Lévesque to speak to them. He finally
accepted, when they were having a convention at Quebec.
But the Women's Canadian Club of Quebec knew that

---

[2] Father Marcel Marcotte, S.J., was at this time Professor in the
Advanced Institute of Religious Sciences and in the Faculty of
Medicine of the University of Montreal. He regarded free education as a socialist-inspired idea. In an article in *Relations* (April
1958) entitled 'About Free Education', he declared: 'That free
education that the best, the most disinterested, the most impatient
among us had gone, too soon, to seek afar—we shall find it, in the
words of the Sage, laid at our doorstep.'

[3] Father Georges-Henri Lévesque. Prime Minister Duplessis had
long made difficulties over subsidies to Laval University because
of Father Lévesque's position there.

Mr Duplessis didn't like Father Lévesque. Consequence:
the Canadian Clubs 'from coast to coast' cancelled the
invitation. Here is the very quintessence of cowardice.
For when some poor devil trades his political liberty for
a job as handyman in a government building, we can
pity him for not having finer feelings. But when well-fed
business men, with the word 'democracy' forever on their
lips, allow the Union Nationale to dictate their choice of
a speaker, we have the right to ask for an explanation.
Until I receive proof to the contrary, I refuse to believe
that in future one single man of honour will attend one of
these famous Canadian Club luncheons—now that I
know that you have to check your liberty at the door
before sitting down to your humble pie.

16 When the people are in power

Human governments . . . derive their origin and their power from the people themselves; in fact, the people— unless prevented by violence or fraud—are free by natural right, and it is they who endow their leaders with the powers they consider suitable.   CARDINAL CAJETAN

The people are free, and can be ruled only so far as they agree to obey, as I have shown. And I have drawn the conclusion that the people have a perfect right to throw out those who hold political authority over them.

It follows that one cannot speak of the duty of obedience without coupling with it the right of revolt. It is this contingent right that constitutes the surest bulwark against tyranny; for the authorities can take assurance from it that, the greater their oppression, the more transitory will be their power.

In this connection, it is deplorable that history as it has been taught among us treats the great revolutions (French, Russian, etc.) only in terms of their ill effects and never acknowledges that it is possible to see them as struggles for liberty against injustice. As a result it has given our people a morality in which insubordination is synonymous with infamy, and authority with infallibility.

In reality, though, the first thing to ask of history is that it should point out to us the paths of liberty. The great lesson to draw from revolutions is not that they devour humanity but rather that tyranny never fails to generate them.

Ten to one there will be some imbeciles who will deduce from those paragraphs that I am preaching revolution, just as there were some who asserted that I was recommending political assassination. It is worth repeating, then: I am against violence. And it is precisely in order to forestall it that I have examined the conditions in which it usually breaks out. It is a fact that people sometimes have to fight to defend their liberty; but I should greatly prefer that it were never attacked, and it is to that end that these articles recommend a politics without tyranny. If that is to have a revolutionary spirit, then I admit to it, but I must add that such a spirit is the best safeguard against revolution.

Our study of politics leads us, then, to pose this problem: what régime, or what system, gives the maximum guarantee against oppression? Given these terms of reference, our investigation can dispense with a comparative study of various forms of government. True, a monarchy can offer more continuity than a republic, and a dictatorship gives (temporary) guarantees of order that a democracy cannot match. But that is not our problem. In itself it is of little importance to purge our souls of violence; what matters is to make it useless by seeing to it that liberty always has peaceful means of expressing itself.

A possible reply here would be that it is conceivable that a benevolent despot might rule wisely, establish a just order for all his subjects, and leave them enough freedom of expression. Would such a régime not be based on the consent of the people?

Yes, this is conceivable. But such consent clearly could not be taken for granted. A mechanism would have to be provided to allow the people to express their opinions freely on the excellence of the régime and the wisdom of the despot. There would also have to be some device to ensure that the despot would abdicate if opinion went against him. And finally a means would have to be invented to designate, peacefully, a successor whom the people would agree to obey. But clearly such a régime would no longer be called a despotism; it would have borrowed the actual mechanism of democracy.

And it must be recognized that democracy is the form of government we are looking for. It is the system in which popular consent is most methodically sought; it is the one that allows the people to choose and dismiss their rulers as peacefully as possible.

But that is not all. It is all very well that a régime should be capable of suppressing the things that cause coups d'état, revolts, and civil wars. That is in a sense the negative side of a government based on popular consent. But liberty is more creative than that, and it is more important that a régime should be able to profit from it in a positive manner. It is in this respect that democracy succeeds better than any other form of government, as I hope to explain in my next article.

17 Contempt of the legislature

If the people are silent, you call them content; if they protest you say that they are given to disorder; and in the one case as in the other they can look to you for nothing.

GLADSTONE

Democracy is superior to other political systems, as I have explained, because it solicits the express agreement of the people and thus avoids the necessity of violent changes. At each election, in fact, the people assert their liberty by deciding what government they will consent to obey.

Hence we must shun the concept of the state as a machine to command obedience and impose order. The truly democratic state should rather *court* obedience and serve the citizens' loyalty by maintaining an order that they will think just. Under these conditions the exercise of force (army, police, prison) cannot become a *habit* of government. My idea of a state 'made to measure' applies thoroughly here: the state must use force only to the extent that individuals or organizations try to use it themselves against the common good. If it is true that in the last analysis the state must retain the monopoly of force, the purpose is less to use it than to prevent someone else from usurping the thunderbolts.

The detractors of democracy are wrong, then, in equating this form of government with anarchy, disorder, and impotence. The democratic state is a strong state; but its strength, being based on agreement, can be exerted only in the direction desired by the consensus of citizens.

Now, what is it that the citizens desire? That is the question that every democratic government must ask itself constantly. And it is in this respect that the democratic state, better than any other, turns to account the creative liberty of people living in society. For if it is to establish an order that citizens will agree to support, the state must go further than merely investigating their needs; it must also encourage them to demand what they consider just. In this way democracy becomes a system in which all citizens *participate* in government: the laws, in a sense, reflect the wishes of the citizens and thus turn to account the special wisdom of each one; the social order to some extent embodies all the wealth of human experience that the citizens possess.

In such a state the liberty of citizens is an end in itself. The authorities don't think of it as an annoying phrase; on the contrary, they want it, and encourage it as the surest guide to the common good.

And that defines just how remote from the democratic spirit are the political *mores* of Quebec. With very few exceptions, and at any level of authority you care to pick, you find only distrust of freedom and hostility towards its exercise. Thus the people are trapped in the dilemma Gladstone was talking about: if they suffer in silence, the authorities think, 'Here's a nice little society, content with its low wages, its slums, and its ignorance'; and if they dare to complain they are blamed for succumbing to the agitation of dangerous 'leftists'.

The government that goes by the name of Union Nationale is the manifest master of this technique; it stands supreme in its contempt for freedom. It is not merely that it spits on the right of association (the anti-union laws), harasses free speech (the padlock law), despises human dignity (beatings by the provincial police), but, more than all this, it insults the spirit of democracy in its most solemn sanctuary, the parliament. I hold no brief for the Liberal opposition—on the contrary its mediocrity is partly to blame for the ills we suffer. But I choke with indignation at the humiliations inflicted on that opposition. The point is that in a parliamentary democracy the opposition is the last and most important bulwark against arbitrary tyranny; through it the people reserve the right to criticize from moment to moment the way they are governed—through it they nip legislative and administrative abuses in the bud. And the Duplessis government, by buffoonery, contempt, accusation, insult, intimidation, illegality, and fraud, has prevented the parliamentary opposition from performing its functions and has therefore gagged the people in the persons of their best-accredited representatives. If it is alleged that these words constitute contempt of the legislature, I can always be summoned to appear at the bar of the assembly. And they will learn that a free citizen does not suffer without protest the degradation of his liberties.   *142187*

18 The right of protest

We hold these truths to be self-evident, that all men are created equal, that they are endowed by their Creator with certain unalienable rights, that among these are life, liberty, and the pursuit of happiness. DECLARATION OF INDEPENDENCE

We have seen that the truly democratic state is bound to encourage the exercise of freedom among its citizens so that, by listening to them, it may learn better what paths to follow to attain the common good.

That is why certain political rights are inseparable from the very essence of democracy: freedom of thought, speech, expression (in the press, on the radio, etc.), assembly, and association. Indeed, the moment these freedoms suffer the smallest restraint, the citizens have lost their full power to participate in the organization of the social order. And so that each citizen may feel the benefit of the inalienable right to exercise his liberties—in spite of anyone, in spite of the state itself—to these rights two more must be added: equality of all before the law, and the right not to be deprived of one's liberty or one's goods without recourse to a trial before one's peers, under an impartial and independent judicial system.

The rights listed in the last paragraph are so basic that they are regarded in democratic philosophy as inalienable —that is, to assure the effective participation of all citizens in the development of public policy, these rights must remain vested in each citizen independently of the laws. To guarantee that they will remain beyond the reach of the state, many democratic constitutions have felt the need to include a 'bill of rights', treating these rights as in some sense anterior to the very existence of the state.

This is not, alas, the case with us. However, the fact that Canada is a federal country, in which sovereignty is shared between a central government and provincial governments, has enabled the Supreme Court to invalidate certain laws as infringing on civil liberties. Thus the court annulled the laws diminishing the freedom of the press in Alberta several years ago; and, more recently, the padlock law restricting the diffusion of political ideas and the bylaw restricting the diffusion of religious ideas (in the Jehovah's Witnesses affair[1]). In a similar context, the court also invalidated the Labour Relations Board's action in revoking the certification of the Teachers' Alliance without giving the parties a hearing.

But neither the Supreme Court nor even a bill of rights can protect us against the lack of democracy in our own thinking. As I said last week, hostility to political freedom reigns in Quebec. I have described the rape of the opposition's liberties in the legislative assembly itself;

---

[1] Persecuted by Mr Duplessis, the Jehovah's Witnesses appealed to the Supreme Court. Mr Roncarelli, a Montreal restaurant-owner who was a member of the sect, undertook the expenses of the suit. Mr Duplessis arbitrarily took away his licence to sell alcohol, which was likely to ruin his business. Mr Roncarelli sued the prime minister and was awarded $33,000 damages and costs.

and the extra-parliamentary opposition is still more sav-
agely attacked: see the Picard,[2] Guindon,[3] and DesMarais[4] bills.

It is a serious matter when the government attacks our
inalienable rights, whether by laws or by executive
action. It is still more serious when citizens, through
cowardice or stupidity, relinquish their rights even when
not required by law to do so.

No law forbids trade-unionists to march on Quebec
City; or the students of Laval to help the Asbestos workers; or a professor to publish a book on federalism; or
university students to boycott lectures or the three to
approach the prime minister. Not only are these actions
legal, but the very logic of democracy demands that they
should be taken, by citizens who wish to participate in
the destinies of the nation. That is not to say that everyone ought to have agreed with the objects of these
actions; but everyone ought to have acknowledged the
principle that they were permissible.

In fact they were condemned, and denounced as revo-

---

[2] The well-known trade-unionist Gérard Picard was not in Mr
Duplessis's good graces. About 1952, the provincial police rather
arbitrarily arrested him at Saint-Janvier for speeding, and the
court suspended his driver's licence. But it happened that, as well
as his driver's licence, Mr Picard had a chauffeur's licence in the
name of J. Pierre G. Picard. He went on driving his car; but a few
days later the provincial police arrested him again as he was
leaving Quebec City. After examining the second permit, the police
had to let him go. Mr Duplessis then added to the Motor Vehicles
Act a retroactive clause requiring those who held two permits to
surrender both in the event of a violation. As the law was retroactive, Mr Picard had to give in and have recourse to a chauffeur
to go about his business as President of the Confederation of
National Trade Unions.

[3] The 'Guindon Bill', passed in 1954 but retroactive to 1944, had
the effect of making illegal all the union activity during that period
of Léo Guindon, President of the Teachers' Alliance of Montreal.

[4] For the 'DesMarais Bill', see p. 49n.

lutionary, in the very quarters that ought to have been most concerned to preserve basic freedoms: the university and the press. Prelates, rectors, deans, and professors abused their authority when they tried to prevent these actions by intimidation or denunciation. And some newspapers saw in them the first signs of the approaching revolution.

Here I want to denounce, quite specifically, the Quebec *Soleil* and *Montréal-Matin*. At the time of the convention of the National Federation of Canadian University Students last October, I launched the idea of a students' strike. Forthwith, in articles taking issue with me personally, the anonymous leader-writers of these alleged journals of information (!) cried 'illegality' and 'rebellion', and declared that 'student strikes and [labour] marches are a form of provocation of authority'. It seemed to me that these newspapers held freedom cheap; but when I wrote to them to demand correction of certain false accusations they had made against me, I learned that they held honour just as cheap. They turned a deaf ear, counting no doubt on my not having the patience to go on attacking their potent anonymity.

Mr Léopold Richer of *Notre-Temps* also thought good to copy the stupidities of *Le Soleil* on his own account. But he edits a journal of opinion. Since by definition his opinions are not those of his opponents, I think his attack on me is perfectly fair fighting. This gentleman is not always logical; he doesn't always make good sense; but I honour him that he at least has the courage to sign his articles.

As for *Le Soleil* and *Montréal-Matin*, I know neither the owners, nor the editors, nor the leader-writers. But, anonymous as they are, I take much pleasure in informing them—if they don't know it already—that they are members of a fine crew of liars and cowards.

19 St Thomas agrees with Karl Marx

Our object in founding the state was not the unbounded happiness of any one class, but the greatest happiness of all; we thought that in a state ordered with a view to the general welfare we would have more chance of discovering justice. PLATO

These principles laid down by Plato twenty-three centuries ago remain true today. The aim of life in society is the greatest happiness of everyone, and this happiness is attained only by rendering justice to each person.

We have seen that democracy tends towards the good of the community by encouraging each citizen and each group of citizens to protest against the defects of society and to demand justice.

A state enlightened in this way can then play its part, which is to protect the rights of every individual, and especially of the weak. This function of the state is indispensable above all in a modern society like ours, where the citizen is in greater danger of becoming enmeshed in a network of extremely complicated social, economic, and administrative institutions. The ordinary citizen has neither the time nor the means to make sure whether a certain public utility is charging him fair rates, whether a certain monopoly is selling to him at reasonable prices, whether a certain cartel or a certain company is not exploiting him to death. And even if the citizen knew that he was the victim of injustice he would not have the power to attack the guilty.

So if the citizen wants to avoid being ordered about against his will, he must provide himself with a protector in the form of a state strong enough to subordinate to the public good all the individuals and organisms that go to make up society. That is why, as well as possessing (as I said in earlier chapters) the monopoly on physical force, the state must assure itself of the services of capable men, rivalling in competence and devotion the best specialists in industry, commerce, and the professions: without that, it is impossible to ensure the triumph of the public over the private good.

Besides, as long as the Quebec state is not equipped with a civil service that is really up to its job, it cannot be hoped that the state will protect the public good adequately in its thousand-and-one negotiations with other states (in fiscal agreements, for instance) or with private interests (as in the case of companies exploiting our natural resources).

To be sure, these problems are common to all countries, whether they are democratic or not. Everywhere in the modern world strong states and competent administrations are required. But, once given these, democracy regains its advantage, for it alone offers the means of using this strength and this competence always for the general good and not for a special interest. What use is it to have civil servants capable of subordinating economic and social institutions to the common good if the political leaders don't want it? Too often the state appears as an instrument in the hands of powerful special interests, rather than as an arbiter trying to render to each his

due. Thus, Karl Marx saw the state as a tool whereby
the capitalist class exploited the working class. And three
centuries earlier St Thomas More had said: 'Therfore
when I consider . . . all these commen wealthes . . . I can
perceave nothing but a certein conspiracy of riche men
procuringe their owne commodities under the name and
title of the commen wealth.' And if anyone fears that
these are Communist principles, or at any rate too remote
to be true, let him consult the joint pastoral letter of the
archbishops and bishops of the province of Quebec in
1941: 'Anyone who took the trouble to examine one by
one the laws passed by the federal parliament or by our
provincial legislatures over the last fifty years would see
in them principally, it must be admitted, the influence of
high finance and concern to protect private interests. . . .
Capitalism in our country exploits the worker, and our
legislation fails to protect him sufficiently.'

It seems, then, that at all times and under all systems
there is a tendency for the few to use the state to enslave
the many. For this, too, democracy appears to us the only
possible remedy, since it is the system in which the
citizen consents to be governed by a body of laws that
the *majority* of citizens wanted. Universal suffrage invites
all adult citizens to express themselves on the value of
the laws and the competence and honesty of those who
make them.

If such a system is to function, one clearly has to begin
by believing in it. But official Quebec teaching has long
taken pleasure in underlining the weaknesses of democracy, after having thrown sand in its works itself. I have
before me a philosophy textbook used in our church high
schools: it teaches distrust of universal suffrage. Under
these circumstances it is very naïve to be surprised that
democracy among us should be so slow in getting started.

20 For a living democracy

I know no safe depository of the ultimate powers of the society but the people themselves; and if we think them not enlightened enough to exercise their control with a wholesome discretion, the remedy is not to take it from them, but to inform their discretion.   THOMAS JEFFERSON

At the end of this first series of articles, which is based on the Declaration of Principles of the Rassemblement,[1] democracy appears as the logical outcome of a policy aimed at preventing tyranny, avoiding violence, doing justice to all, encouraging the full flowering of personality, and turning to account the creative liberty of every citizen.

That is not to say that democracy is a perfect form of government: you just have to look around you . . . What holds us to democracy is not that it is faultless but that it is less faulty than any other system. If the people use their sovereignty badly, the remedy is not to take it away from them (for to whom could we hand it over who would offer a better guarantee for *all* citizens?), but rather to educate them to do better. To be precise, democracy is the only form of government that fully respects the dignity of man, because it alone is based on the belief that all men can be made fit to participate, directly or

[1] See Prof. Cook's introduction, p. 14.

indirectly, in the guidance of the society of which they are members.

However, we must refrain from making undue claims for democracy; that would be the best way to discredit it. For instance, democracy does not claim that majority rule is an infallible guide to *truth*. Nor does it claim that the average citizen is capable of resolving the extraordinarily complicated problems that face modern governments.

As for majority rule, the fact must be faced that it is a convention, possessing simply a practical value. It is convenient to choose governments and pass laws by majority vote, so that those who exercise authority can feel assured of having more supporters than opponents —which is in itself some guarantee that the social order will be upheld. It is true that from one point of view the majority convention is only a roundabout way of applying the law of the stronger, in the form of the law of the more numerous. Let us admit it, but note at the same time that human groupings took a great step towards civilization when they agreed to justify their actions by counting heads instead of breaking them.

And this must be added. Democracy genuinely demonstrates its faith in man by letting itself be guided by the rule of fifty-one per cent. For if all men are equal, each one the possessor of a special dignity, it follows inevitably that the happiness of fifty-one people is more important than that of forty-nine; it is normal, then, that —*ceteris paribus* and taking account of the inviolable rights of the minority—the decisions preferred by the fifty-one should prevail. But the majority convention has only a practical value, I repeat. Democracy recognizes that one person may be right and ninety-nine wrong. That is why freedom of speech is sacred: the one person must always have the right to proclaim *his* truth in the hope of persuading the ninety-nine to change their point of view.

On the second claim falsely attributed to democracy, the point is that parliamentary democracy does not require a decision from its subjects on each of the technical problems presented by the complicated art of government in the modern world. It would be a delusion to look to a vote of the citizens to settle the details of, for example, a fiscal policy, a war budget, or a diplomatic mission. The citizens as a group can judge such measures only by their effects—real or apparent—on the happiness of the group.

That is why modern democracies hardly ever resort to the plebiscite—which requires each citizen to decide on what is often too technical a question. In contrast, the electoral system asks of the citizen only that he should decide on a set of ideas and tendencies, and on men who can hold them and give effect to them. These sets of ideas and men constitute political parties, which are indispensable for the functioning of parliamentary democracy.

But the study of parties, and of their responsibilities in the democratic education of citizens and in the guidance of the nation, opens up a new direction for our approaches . . .